DANNY DEVITO

An Acting Legend's Memoir - From Broadway to Hollywood

Harvey L. Green

All rights reserved. No part of this publication may be reproduced, distributed, or transmitted in any form or by any means, including photocopying, recording, or other electronic or mechanical method, without the prior written permission of the publisher, except in the case of brief quotations embodied in critical reviews and certain other noncommercial uses permitted by the copyright law.

Copyright ©Harvey L. Green, 2024

TABLE OF CONTENTS

INTRODUCTION

CHAPTER 1: WHO IS DANNY DEVITO.

Childhood

Education

Background

CHAPTER TWO: BROADWAY'S ORIGINS

CHAPTER 3: HOLLYWOOD TRANSITION

Taxi and Beyond

CHAPTER 4: SCENES FROM BELOW

Producing and directing

CHAPTER 5: RELATIONS WITH FAMILY

Partnership

CHAPTER 6: OBSTACLES AND SUCCESSES

An Honest Introspection

CHAPTER 7: NOTABLE POSITIONS

Famous Times

CHAPTER 8: THE ENTERTAINMENT INDUSTRY'S LEGACY AND ITS IMPACT

Funny Smarts

Vision for the film

Philanthropic activities

CONCLUSION

INTRODUCTION

Come along with me as I take you through the life and career of Danny DeVito, one of Hollywood's most adored characters, in this memoir. This book provides an insight into the adventures, successes, and setbacks that have defined my career in the entertainment world, from his modest beginnings to becoming a household celebrity. From Broadway to Hollywood, I urge you to learn about the man behind the legendary roles via open contemplation and personal tales. Come along as we discuss the smiles, sobs, and life-changing events that have shaped my career as an actor, producer, and director. Greetings from Danny DeVito's world.

Greetings from the pages of my life, where writing has been my passion and the stage and film my canvas. I pull back the curtain on my trip from the busy streets of New York City to the glitz and glamour of Hollywood in these chapters. You will discover the experiences that have molded me into an actor, director, and supporter of the arts as you flip each page. This book provides an honest depiction of the highs and lows of a life lived in the spotlight, from the early days of fighting to make ends meet to the height of success. Come along as I share my memories of the people I met, the connections I built, and the lessons I discovered along the road. It's time for you to enter Danny DeVito's world, mine.

CHAPTER 1: WHO IS DANNY DEVITO.

American actor, director, and producer Danny DeVito is well-known for his varied skill set and striking appearance. As Louie De Palma in the television series "Taxi" in the late 1970s and early 1980s, he became well-known. Starring in several movies, DeVito's credits include "Romancing the Stone," "One Flew Over the Cuckoo's Nest," "Twins," "Batman Returns," and "Matilda." In addition to performing, he has produced several motion pictures and television series and directed several popular films. Thanks to his services to the entertainment business, DeVito has gained recognition and a devoted following.

Childhood

On November 17, 1944, in Neptune Township, New Jersey, USA, Danny DeVito was born. DeVito was raised in a modest Italian-American home and at an early age realized he had a talent for performing. Despite his small size, he accepted his individuality and became very interested in theater and storytelling.

Following high school graduation, DeVito went to New York City to study acting at the American Academy of Dramatic Arts. Before making his debut in movies and television, he developed his skills on stage by participating in several off-Broadway musicals.

DeVito's early years were characterized by tenacity and resolve as he made his way through the cutthroat entertainment industry. His early experiences would influence his professional path and make him a highly skilled individual in the field.

Education

During his early years, Danny DeVito attended Oratory Prep School and Our Lady of Mount Carmel School in New Jersey. Upon graduating from high school, he enrolled at the American Academy of Dramatic Arts in New York City to further his acting passion. It was there that he had official training in acting and theater, which prepared him for a lucrative career in show business. In addition to giving him the abilities and methods he needed, DeVito's education gave him a profound respect for the storytelling and performance arts.

Background

In Neptune Township, New Jersey, Danny DeVito was born into an Italian-American family. Julia and Daniel DeVito Sr., his parents, had a little company. DeVito was raised in a close-knit community and was impacted by his family's history as a child.

Despite having to overcome obstacles as a young child because of his diminutive stature, DeVito accepted his individuality and acquired a strong mindset. He had a strong work ethic and a strong sense of dedication from his upbringing, which would help him in his pursuit of an acting career.

DeVito has always maintained a strong connection to his heritage, frequently using his childhood as an inspiration for his work as an actor, director, and producer. His upbringing has greatly influenced how he approaches storytelling in the entertainment business and how he defines himself.

CHAPTER TWO: BROADWAY'S ORIGINS

Broadway stages served as the starting point of Danny DeVito's career in entertainment. Following his education at the American Academy of Dramatic Arts, DeVito entered the theatrical industry, showcasing his range and skill as an actor.

Early Broadway roles helped DeVito become known and establish himself as a potential artist. His skill was refined in plays like "The Man with the Flower in His Mouth" and "One Flew Over the Cuckoo's Nest," which brought him praise from critics and prepared him for his move to television and film.

In addition to gaining invaluable knowledge, DeVito's Broadway endeavors shaped his storytelling and performance style by collaborating with renowned directors and actors.

DeVito's future success in Hollywood and other areas would be firmly based on the skills he gained during his Broadway debut.

Industry insiders saw Danny DeVito's talent and commitment to his art during his Broadway tenure. His performances attracted a devoted audience as well as praise from critics due to his singular combination of charm, wit, and sincerity.

DeVito's Broadway career began with a string of noteworthy parts that demonstrated his versatility as an actor. He proved that he could hold an audience's attention with his captivating performances, whether he was playing humorous or difficult serious roles.

Outside of the spotlight, DeVito worked with other actors, directors, and playwrights in New York City's thriving theater community. Every performance he was a part of demonstrated his love for the theater and dedication to perfection.

When DeVito moved to the world of cinema and television, where he would continue to create an enduring impression on the entertainment business, the lessons he had learned and the relationships he had built during his Broadway days would prove crucial.

During his tenure on Broadway, DeVito was able to hone his acting abilities in addition to being able to show off his talent. He fully engaged himself in the theatrical community, picking up tips from seasoned pros and taking in the subtleties of the trade.

Through his Broadway adventures, he was exposed to a wide range of theatrical genres and styles, from avant-garde experimental shows to beloved classics. DeVito took on parts that stretched the limits of his skills and forced him to develop as an actor, which tested his adaptability as a performer.

A spirit of camaraderie among the cast and crew was also cultivated by the collaborative nature of theater production, forging enduring friendships and business relationships that would influence DeVito's career for years to come.

Looking back, DeVito's Broadway days set the stage for his later success in movies and television by giving him a strong base of knowledge, skill, and creative vision.

CHAPTER 3: HOLLYWOOD TRANSITION

Danny DeVito made his name for himself on Broadway and then aimed to take over Hollywood. He made a smooth transition from the stage to the big screen thanks to his special combination of talent, charisma, and distinct presence. He soon rose to the top of the acting world.

In the highly regarded film "One Flew Over the Cuckoo's Nest" (1975), DeVito landed his breakthrough role as the cunning and manipulative prisoner Martini, giving an unforgettable performance. In addition to showcasing his acting abilities, this role gave him access to a plethora of Hollywood options.

DeVito cemented his reputation as a versatile actor in the 1980s and 1990s by appearing in a wide variety of genre-spanning films. His acting career spanned comedies such as "Romancing the Stone" (1984) and "Twins" (1988) to dramas like "Terms of Endearment" (1983) and "War of the Roses" (1989), showcasing his exceptional timing and nuanced character development.

DeVito expanded his acting career by pursuing endeavors in directing and producing, so solidifying his status as a versatile performer in the entertainment sector. His first feature film, "Throw Momma from the Train" (1987), won him praise from critics and opened doors for other directing endeavors. It also demonstrated his talent for dark humor and narrative.

DeVito faced many difficulties during his move to Hollywood, but his unyielding perseverance and unquestionable talent helped him overcome these setbacks and achieve unmatched success in the film and television industries. His transition from Broadway to Hollywood is evidence of his love of narrative and his continuing influence as a major figure in American film.

Danny DeVito's distinct combination of charm, wit, and adaptability won him over to both viewers and directors as he made the move to Hollywood. His ability to play a variety of characters with ease, from endearing eccentrics to terrifying villains, made him a highly sought-after talent in the business.

DeVito's turns in classic movies like "Ruthless People" (1986) and "The War of the Roses" (1989), where his signature comedy and perfect timing stole the show, cemented his reputation as a comic powerhouse throughout the 1980s. Concurrently, he showcased his acting range in critically acclaimed dramas such as "The Rainmaker" (1997) and "Tin Men" (1987), displaying his dramatic prowess.

Working on multiple movies with director Tim Burton, such as "Batman Returns" (1992) and "Big Fish" (2003), was one of DeVito's most memorable partnerships. Burton's inventive storytelling was wonderfully complemented by DeVito's larger-than-life presence and natural ability to inhabit oddball characters, creating unique cinematic experiences.

Along with his accomplishments in front of the camera, DeVito was a successful producer and director behind the scenes. He became even more of a Hollywood heavyweight when his production firm, Jersey Films, brought box office hits including "Pulp Fiction" (1994) and "Erin Brockovich" (2000).

Danny DeVito's move to Hollywood was marked by a career-long dedication to pushing the limits of his profession and a ceaseless pursuit of perfection. His work on television and movies has had a lasting impact on the business, cementing his reputation as one of Hollywood's most cherished and durable talents.

Taxi and Beyond

Being Louie De Palma in the TV show "Taxi" launched Danny DeVito to fame and solidified his legacy in the annals of television history. With his larger-than-life performance and perfect comedic timing, DeVito enthralled audiences as the sarcastic but strangely appealing dispatcher of the Sunshine Cab Company.

The 1978–1983 television series "Taxi" highlighted DeVito's extraordinary skill as an actor and comic. Along with receiving a lot of praise, he won a Golden Globe and an Emmy for Best Supporting Actor in a Comedy Series for his portrayal of Louie De Palma.

After "Taxi," DeVito's career took off and he moved between film and television with ease. He made appearances in a wide range of films, including comedies like "Twins" (1988) and "Throw Momma from the Train" (1987) and tragedies like "Hoffa" (1992) and "L.A. Confidential" (1997).

Apart from his acting career, DeVito also dabbled in directing and producing, so reinforcing his standing as a versatile artist in the entertainment sector. His directing endeavors, such as "Matilda" (1996) and "The War of the Roses" (1989), demonstrated his mastery of storytelling and distinct vision.

Although "Taxi" catalyzed Danny DeVito's rise to fame, his contributions to cinema and television have made it clear that his influence goes well beyond the Sunshine Cab Company. DeVito has had a great influence on the entertainment business, from his legendary performances to his behind-the-scenes efforts as a producer and director.

Danny DeVito pushed the limits of his career after landing his breakthrough part in "Taxi," taking on a variety of parts and endeavors that demonstrated his flexibility as an actor and performer.

In the years that followed "Taxi," DeVito became well-known for his roles in television and movies. In comedies like "The Jewel of the Nile" (1985) and "Man on the Moon" (1999), he brought his signature charm and humor to the big screen, giving each character he played more nuance and complexity.

DeVito's creative abilities went beyond his job in front of the camera and included producing and directing. He directed several popular movies, such as "Death to Smoochy" (2002) and "The War of the Roses" (1989), exhibiting his talent for writing compelling stories and motivating his team members.

Along with his successes in movies, DeVito was a well-known figure on television, making memorable cameos on series like "Friends" and "It's Always Sunny in Philadelphia," where his exuberant demeanor and comedic timing were always a hit.

As a result of his lasting contributions to the entertainment industry, Danny DeVito has established himself as a very flexible and resilient talent throughout his career, winning over fans worldwide. DeVito's legacy is a monument to his enthusiasm, commitment, and unmatched talent as an actor and entertainer, from his legendary role in "Taxi" to his multiple on-stage and film triumphs.

CHAPTER 4: SCENES FROM BELOW

Outside of the spotlight, Danny DeVito had a significant influence on the entertainment business that went well beyond his on-screen roles. He became a creative force behind the scenes, making a lasting impression as a producer, director, and supporter of independent filmmaking.

Director DeVito brought a unique perspective to every production he oversaw, with a strong grasp of storytelling and visual composition. His ability to combine dark comedy with heartbreaking drama was on display in movies like "Death to Smoochy" (2002) and "Throw Momma from the Train" (1987), which garnered him critical acclaim and cemented his reputation as a versatile director.

Along with his work in front of the camera, DeVito was a producer who supported fresh perspectives and inventive narratives in Hollywood. He guided successful films including "Pulp Fiction" (1994) and "Erin Brockovich" (2000) through his production firm, Jersey Films, and received praise and acclaim for his dedication to high-caliber cinematography.

In addition to his artistic pursuits, DeVito utilized his position to promote social justice and environmental preservation campaigns. His philanthropy and activism have left a lasting impression, encouraging other members of the profession to use their power for good.

Danny DeVito's behind-the-scenes work has been just as important to his career in every way as his on-screen performances. His commitment to quality and his love of creating stories have influenced the direction of film and television for future generations.

Apart from his triumph as an actor, Danny DeVito's unseen efforts have been crucial in molding the entertainment industry's terrain.

As a director, DeVito demonstrated his versatility and competence behind the camera by bringing his distinct viewpoint and imaginative vision to a range of films. Critics and audiences praised him for his directorial debut, "Throw Momma from the Train" (1987), which demonstrated his ability to merge dark comedy with poignant moments. The films "The War of the Roses" (1989) and "Matilda" (1996), among others, cemented his standing as a gifted director with a unique style.

Apart from his directorial endeavors, DeVito has also made noteworthy contributions as a producer, enabling the realization of multiple projects via his production firm, Jersey Films. Production credentials for DeVito range from box office hits like "Man on the Moon" (1999) to indie darlings like "Pulp Fiction" (1994). These credits show his dedication to promoting strong narratives and helping up-and-coming talent in the business.

Moreover, DeVito's support of social causes goes beyond his roles in television and movies. He has used his platform to spread awareness and bring about constructive change in the globe, speaking out in favor of social justice and environmental conservation.

Danny DeVito has created a lasting legacy that goes beyond the screen with his diverse career and commitment to his principles and art. His uncredited work in the background has improved the entertainment sector and encouraged others to use their gifts for the greater benefit.

Producing and directing

Danny DeVito's skill set goes beyond his on-screen persona; he is also a talented filmmaker and producer. His production endeavors allowed him to support intriguing projects and up-and-coming talent in the business, while his directing endeavors allowed him to demonstrate his distinct vision and narrative skills.

As a filmmaker, DeVito has directed a wide range of movies that highlight his adaptability and depth. His directing debut, "Throw Momma from the Train" (1987), won him praise from critics and established him as a formidable force behind the camera. It showcased his talent for fusing sad moments with dark humor. His subsequent directing endeavors, including "Matilda" (1996) and "The War of the Roses" (1989), cemented his standing as a director possessing a unique style and an acute sense of narrative.

Through his production firm, Jersey Films, DeVito has made important contributions as a producer in addition to his directing career. Jersey Films, which was founded in 1991 by Michael Shamberg and Stacey Sher, has produced a variety of films and television shows. From commercial hits like "Erin Brockovich" (2000) to indie darlings like "Pulp Fiction" (1994), Jersey Films has received both critical and financial success, demonstrating DeVito's dedication to promoting strong storytelling and developing new talent in the business.

Danny DeVito has made a lasting impact on the entertainment business as a director and producer, demonstrating his skill as a storyteller and his commitment to promoting originality and creativity in the filmmaking process.

CHAPTER 5: RELATIONS WITH FAMILY

Danny DeVito is an Italian-American with a close-knit family. He was born in Neptune Township, New Jersey, to parents Julia and Daniel DeVito Sr. Theresa and Angela are the two elder sisters of DeVito.

The three children that DeVito and actress Rhea Perlman share, Lucy, Grace, and Jacob, were born in 1982. Perlman is best known for playing Carla Tortelli on the television show "Cheers."

DeVito's family's affection and support have kept him grounded throughout his career. He prioritizes family values and upholds close relationships with his wife and children, even in the face of the pressures of his career.

Partnership

Danny DeVito's personal life has been famous for his connection with actress Rhea Perlman. Soon after they first met in 1971, the pair started dating. They became one of Hollywood's most enduring pairs after getting married in 1982 and staying together for several decades.

Mutual respect, affection, and support for one another's careers defined their partnership. Despite having demanding acting careers, DeVito and Perlman never wavered in their commitment to their family and their close relationship.

However, after almost 30 years of marriage, DeVito and Perlman announced their split in 2012. They nevertheless got along well and have been co-parenting their three kids despite this.

Their union serves as a poignant reminder of the difficulties associated with love and marriage in the entertainment sector, where high demands on schedules and public attention can cause personal relationships to suffer. DeVito and Perlman's unwavering love and dedication to their family, despite their difficulties, serve as a monument to the depth of their bond.

CHAPTER 6: OBSTACLES AND SUCCESSES

Danny DeVito has had several successes that have cemented his place as an industry icon despite the personal and professional setbacks he has endured throughout his life and career.

Overcoming discrimination and prejudices because of his small stature was one of the difficulties DeVito encountered early in his career. Despite this, he chose not to let his height limit him and instead concentrated on developing his acting skills, eventually becoming well-known for being a versatile actor who could play a variety of characters.

Navigating the competitive and frequently unexpected nature of the entertainment industry was another difficulty DeVito faced. He persisted in the face of obstacles and failures, viewing each as a chance for personal development.

Despite the difficulties he encountered, DeVito has had several successes and accomplishments throughout his career. He has continuously pushed the limits of his craft and received praise for his contributions to film and television, starting with his breakthrough performance in "Taxi" and continuing with his success as a director and producer.

In addition, DeVito's lasting appeal and cultural influence have cemented his standing as an industry icon. His unique character, unforgettable performances, and uncompromising commitment to his art have made him a beloved figure to audiences worldwide, guaranteeing that his legacy will last for many more decades.

Ultimately, Danny DeVito's career has been marked by both setbacks and victories, but he has persevered and grown stronger than ever, and his influence on the entertainment business is immense.

Apart from the obstacles and victories in his professional life, Danny DeVito has also gone through personal hardships and periods of reflection, which have aided in his development as a person and an artist.

The breakup of DeVito's long-term marriage to Rhea Perlman in 2012 was one of his struggles. DeVito has shown resiliency and maturity in the face of hardship by keeping a positive attitude and concentrating on co-parenting their three children despite their separation.

DeVito's struggle with alcoholism, which he publicly discussed and sought treatment for in the 1980s, was another pivotal period in his life. DeVito conquered his addiction with perseverance and help, coming out stronger and with a greater concentration on his professional and personal well-being.

DeVito has had many victories and happy moments in his life despite these obstacles. He has found great joy in his long-lasting friendships and working relationships with other actors and directors, and he has been able to positively influence subjects that are important to him through his activism and charitable endeavors.

DeVito has won over both fans and colleagues with his ability to handle life's highs and lows with grace, humor, and genuineness. Everyone who respects his work and his character finds encouragement in his ability to bounce back from setbacks and his unshakable dedication to his job.

An Honest Introspection

Danny DeVito provides an honest look back at the highs and lows, obstacles, and victories that have molded his life and career. He explores his times of hesitation and doubt as well as the difficulties and failures that tried his resolve and perseverance.

DeVito offers insights into the lessons he has learned along the road, the personal development and self-discovery that have resulted from facing adversity and accepting change, through this open perspective. He celebrates the victories and accomplishments that have made him happy and fulfilled while also acknowledging the errors and stumbles, regrets, and lost chances.

DeVito bares his soul in this introspective investigation, exposing the weaknesses and insecurities that lurk beneath his charismatic exterior. He shares his insights on the intricacies of fame and wealth, the demands and anticipations that accompany public personas, and the significance of remaining loyal to oneself despite the cacophony and diversion of the entertainment sector.

In the end, DeVito's open assessment provides an insight into the mind and spirit of a man who has experienced life to the fullest, welcoming its trials and victories with bravery, wit, and humility. It serves as a monument to the strength of self-reflection and self-awareness and serves as a timely reminder of the importance of resilience and honesty in the search for contentment and pleasure.

Danny DeVito explores the complexities of his career and personal journey in an open meditation, providing an unvarnished and unadulterated story of the events that have molded him.

He gives viewers an insight into the inner workings of Hollywood and the entertainment industry by sharing personal anecdotes and behind-the-scenes tales. DeVito exposes the highs and lows of living in the spotlight, from negotiating auditions and getting breakthrough parts to battling the demands of fame and the public's criticism.

In addition, DeVito considers the bonds that have strengthened his life, ranging from the close bonds he has with his family to the treasured connections he has with other actors and partners. He shares his thoughts on the benefits and drawbacks of children, marriage, and the lasting value of love and connection in the middle of the insanity that is show business.

DeVito gives advice and inspiration to people going through similar difficulties and uncertainty in their own lives through this open perspective. He shares knowledge gained from a lifetime of experience, inspiring readers to believe in the strength of the human spirit and the value of pursuing goals with tenacity.

DeVito's open analysis provides insight, motivation, and a dash of comedy while attesting to the complexity of the human experience. Readers are struck by this intensely personal and emotionally stirring journey, which sticks with them long after the last page is turned.

CHAPTER 7: NOTABLE POSITIONS

Danny DeVito has portrayed a wide range of characters in his successful career that has made a lasting impression on viewers all over the world. His portrayals of anything from endearing eccentrics to frightening villains have enthralled audiences and solidified his reputation as a gifted and legendary actor.

Bringing humor and depth to the character, DeVito won several accolades and critical praise for his portrayal as the cantankerous and cunning dispatcher of the Sunshine Cab Company, Louie De Palma, is one of DeVito's most remembered performances from the television series "Taxi."

DeVito has made remarkable performances in a range of film genres. He demonstrated his ability to play nuanced and morally gray characters in Tim Burton's "Batman Returns" as the cunning and cunning Penguin, and audiences were deeply affected by his depiction of the charming and eccentric Oswald Cobblepot.

DeVito's comedic abilities have also been highlighted in movies such as "Matilda," in which he portrayed the endearing outlaw Harry Wormwood, and "Throw Momma from the Train," in which he played the unfortunate Owen Lift.

DeVito's filmography is replete with standout performances that cover a wide range of human emotions and experiences in addition to these classic parts. Because of DeVito's versatility and acting prowess, every job he plays, whether it be exploring the depths of the human mind or playing characters with larger-than-life personalities, creates an enduring impression on viewers long after the credits have rolled.

Here are a few more iconic roles that Danny DeVito has played:

1. Vincent Benedict in the 1988 comedy "Twins": DeVito costarred with Arnold Schwarzenegger in this film about improbable twins who were split up at birth, demonstrating their amazing chemistry and timing.

Danny DeVito plays streetwise con man Vincent Benedict in the 1988 comedy "Twins," who has a taste for mischief. The character is presented as the long-lost twin brother of Arnold Schwarzenegger's Julius Benedict, who is opposed to Vincent in every manner.

Vincent is shown as a quick-witted hustler who always seems to find himself in problems and who must use cunning and street smarts to get by in the world. Vincent is smaller than his genetically altered twin brother Julius and does not possess his sibling's physical attributes.

Nevertheless, his sharp mind, cunning, and silver tongue make up for his inadequacies.

Vincent provides comic relief with his unusual antics and larger-than-life personality throughout the film, acting as a comical counterpoint to Julius's earnestness and naivety. Though he presents a tough exterior, Vincent is rather vulnerable, and he longs for the sense of community that Julius and his new relationship provide.

A lot of the humor and heart of the picture comes from Vincent's colorful antics and mishaps, which take place as the twins set out on a mission to find their estranged mother and learn the truth about their origins. Vincent is a fascinating and lovable character who creates an impression on viewers because of his dynamic connection with Julius and DeVito's captivating performance.

The role of Vincent Benedict, played by Danny DeVito in "Twins," demonstrates his comedic skill and adaptability as an actor. This gives the character more nuance and complexity and adds to the movie's lasting appeal.

2. Mr. Wormwood in "Matilda" (1996): DeVito starred and directed this version of the well-loved children's book by Roald Dahl, as the cunning and uncaring father of the title character.

Mr. Wormwood in the 1996 film "Matilda":

Danny DeVito plays Harry Wormwood in the 1996 motion picture adaptation of the well-known children's novel "Matilda," which is about the father of the title character, Matilda, who is a cruel and dishonest man. Mr. Wormwood is presented as a sleazy and dishonest used car salesman who is more concerned with his daughter's education and well-being than with making a quick profit.

In his depiction of Mr. Wormwood, DeVito conveys the character's conceit, haughtiness, and lack of empathy, presenting him as a vile person who mistreats Matilda and minimizes her potential. Matilda's passion for reading and her quest for knowledge contrast sharply with Mr. Wormwood's contempt for books and education throughout the movie, laying the groundwork for their eventual confrontation.

Mr. Wormwood's tricks and deceit are revealed when Matilda develops her telekinetic powers and starts to outwit her uncaring parents, ultimately resulting in his downfall. DeVito gives the role a humorous touch, adding charm and fun to his portrayal even in the face of Mr. Wormwood's despicable deeds.

Mr. Wormwood is portrayed with a sense of silliness and exaggeration that contributes to the amusing tone of the picture, despite his wicked character. Mr. Wormwood is a fascinating and engaging enemy, providing the ideal counterpoint to Matilda's bravery and resiliency thanks to DeVito's strong presence and hilarious timing.

As Mr. Wormwood in "Matilda," Danny DeVito demonstrates his ability to provide complexity and nuance to even the most sinister characters, which adds to the film's allure and enduring appeal to viewers of all ages.

3. Larry the Liquidator in "Other People's Money" (1991): DeVito made a striking impression as a cunning corporate thief in this drama, demonstrating his capacity to play characters with gray morality.

In the 1991 motion picture "Other People's Money," Danny DeVito plays Larry the Liquidator, a.k.a. Lawrence Garfield. Lawrence is a merciless corporate raider whose only goal is to buy up failing businesses and sell their assets to raise as much money as possible for himself.

Larry the Liquidator is portrayed by DeVito as having a keen sense of humor, a seductive charisma, and unreserved avarice. As he maneuvers through the competitive world of corporate finance, he radiates confidence and arrogance, outwitting his rivals with cunning and deception.

Larry, the movie's main adversary, personifies the spirit of Wall Street in the 1980s, when corporate raiders were regarded as world masters and greed was praised. DeVito infuses the role with charisma and charm, which makes him both odious and fascinating to watch.

Larry engages in conflict with various characters throughout the movie, such as Gregory Peck's Jorgy, the creator of the company, and Penelope Ann Miller's Kate, his stepdaughter, who are both keen to keep the business safe from Larry's hostile takeover. The struggle between greed and morality is shown with tension and suspense thanks to DeVito's dramatic performance.

Even though Larry the Liquidator is a villain, DeVito gives the character nuance and depth by including moments of contemplation and vulnerability. As the movie goes on, Larry is made to face the repercussions of his choices, which leads to an unexpected and provocative ending.

Danny DeVito plays Larry the Liquidator in "Other People's Money," demonstrating his ability to give even the most ethically dubious characters complexity and sympathy. Larry's charismatic presence and powerful acting make him an unforgettable antagonist who gives the film's examination of corporate greed and ethics more nuance and complexity.

4. Randle McMurphy in "One Flew Over the Cuckoo's Nest" (1975): DeVito's debut performance in the film garnered him critical praise and signaled the start of his prosperous cinematic career as the cheeky and rebellious prisoner in a mental institution.

5. Ralph in "Romancing the Stone" (1984): DeVito demonstrated his ability to inject humor into any part with this outstanding supporting performance as the sly and comic villain in this action-adventure movie.

6. Larry Wilson in "The War of the Roses" (1989): DeVito demonstrated his directing and acting skills by comparing with Michael Douglas and Kathleen Turner in this dark comedy about a brutal divorce.

7. Martin Weir in "Get Shorty" (1995): DeVito brought his trademark charm and wit to the ensemble cast as a self-absorbed actor in this crime-comedy.

8. Big Dan Teague in the Coen Brothers' eccentric comedy "O Brother, Where Art Thou?" (2000): Despite having little screen time, DeVito had a noteworthy cameo as a one-eyed Bible salesman who left a lasting impression.

These parts demonstrate Danny DeVito's breadth and depth as an actor, showcasing his ability to play both humorous and serious parts, and enhancing his standing as a well-liked and esteemed member of the entertainment community.

Famous Times

Throughout his career, Danny DeVito has produced many memorable moments, both on and off film. These incidents have had a profound effect on viewers and have come to represent his name in the entertainment business.

1. The Penguin's Umbrella : DeVito's performance as the Penguin in Tim Burton's "Batman Returns" is replete with iconic moments, but one of the most well-known may be when he unfolds his umbrella to reveal its lethal arsenal, displaying the dark side and sly intelligence of his persona.
Danny DeVito's take on Oswald Cobblepot, aka the Penguin, in Tim Burton's "Batman Returns," is a classic. The Penguin's reveal of his trademark weapon, the Penguin's Umbrella, is one of his most iconic scenes.

In addition to being a destructive tool, the Penguin's umbrella represents the character's deranged nature. The umbrella, with its elegant appearance and lethal potential, is a representation of the Penguin's inventiveness and slyness. As he uses the umbrella with ferocity and accuracy, DeVito lends a scary aura to the role, employing it to take out his adversaries and advance his evil plans.

The Penguin's umbrella is a visual motif that symbolizes the character's duality rather than merely being a weapon. Like the Penguin himself with his top hat and monocle, it seems innocent and harmless at first glance. But beneath its surface is a lethal cache of technology and weapons that echo the Penguin's cunning and cunning nature.

Throughout "Batman Returns," the Penguin's umbrella acts as a constant reminder of his villainous nature and his thirst for dominance. The umbrella is a flexible and strong weapon that demonstrates the penguin's cunning and brutality, whether it is used to shoot targets, launch missiles, or release a swarm of lethal penguins.

In the end, DeVito's portrayal of the Penguin is mostly defined by his use of an umbrella, which gives his performance more nuance and character depth and establishes the Penguin as one of Batman's most recognizable enemies. The umbrella, with its iconic design and lethal powers, endures as a testament to the Penguin's villainy in the annals of film history.

2. Taxi" Taxi : DeVito played Louie De Palma in the television series "Taxi," which included many memorable moments. However, one that sticks out is when he makes his signature insults and jokes from his dispatcher's cage, showcasing the acerbic charm and sharp wit of the character.

3. Throwing Momma Overboard : DeVito's character, Owen Lift, in "Throw Momma from the Train," is known for thinking about killing his controlling mother. This leads to humorous mistakes and misunderstandings that showcase DeVito's skill for dark humor and physical comedy.

In "Throw Momma from the Train," a dark comedy starring Danny DeVito, Owen Lift muses over a nasty scheme sparked by a creative writing assignment. Throughout the movie, the line "Throwing Momma Overboard" appears frequently, signifying Owen's annoyance with his controlling mother, who he believes has stunted his creativity and freedom.

Owen tells Billy Crystal, who plays his writing instructor, about his plan to free himself from his controlling mother as the movie progresses. Owen grows more and more hooked on the idea of doing so. Owen uses the phrase "Throwing Momma Overboard" to express his desire to rebel against his controlling upbringing and take charge of his own life. It has both a physical and figurative connotation.

As Owen Lift struggles with his mixed feelings for his mother and the fallout from his actions, DeVito's portrayal of the character blends sadness and dark humor. "Throwing Momma Overboard" emerges as a pivotal plot point in the movie, propelling the story ahead as Owen's scheme takes on a life of its own.

In the end, DeVito's character in "Throwing Momma from the Train" acts as both a tragic and humorous counterpoint to the film's themes of familial dysfunction, remorse, and redemption. "Throwing Momma Overboard" perfectly captures the darkly comedic tone of the movie and gives DeVito's performance a deeper level of nuance, making it a noteworthy and legendary moment in his career.

4. Matilda's Liberation : In "Matilda," while DeVito plays the crooked and uncaring father Mr. Wormwood, his astute daughter Matilda, played by Mara Wilson, proves to be the equal of his protégé. One classic scene features Matilda defying her father and taking charge of her own life, demonstrating DeVito's talent for portraying nuanced and flawed people.

The repressive force that Danny DeVito's character, Harry Wormwood, in "Matilda," symbolizes is what Mara Wilson's character Matilda has to resist to claim her individuality and embrace her own identity. The main premise of the movie is Matilda's escape from her abusive and uncaring home, and DeVito's portrayal of Harry Wormwood plays a crucial role in emphasizing the difficulties Matilda encounters along the way.

Matilda experiences abuse and neglect from her parents throughout the movie, as they put their self-interest ahead of her welfare. In particular, Harry Wormwood is shown to be a cunning and dishonest figure who minimizes and disregards Matilda's abilities and intelligence. Matilda has to get over his contempt for learning and his indifference to his daughter's emotions to escape his hold on her.

DeVito plays Harry Wormwood in a way that is both humorous and threatening, charmingly embodying the stereotype of the absentee dad. His attempts to undermine Matilda's confidence and establish his power over her are typified by manipulation and gaslighting in their interactions.

But as the movie goes on, Matilda finds her inner fortitude and resiliency, eventually outwitting her parents and experiencing a sense of empowerment and belonging. Her escape from the destructive influence of her family represents her path to freedom and self-discovery and is a testament to her bravery and tenacity.

In "Matilda," Danny DeVito's interpretation of Harry Wormwood acts as a spur to Matilda's freedom, emphasizing the need to speak up against injustice and claim one's agency in the face of difficulty. Harry Wormwood is made memorable and strong by DeVito's powerful performance, which gives the movie's examination of family dynamics and human development more nuance and complexity.

5. The Twins Reunion : In the film "Twins," Vincent Benedict, played by Danny DeVito, reunites with Julius, played by Arnold Schwarzenegger, his long-lost twin brother. This endearing scene of a brotherly reconciliation accentuates DeVito and Schwarzenegger's comic chemistry and gives the humorous plot of the movie more emotional resonance.

In the film "Twins," Arnold Schwarzenegger's character Julius Benedict, the twin brother represented by Danny DeVito's character, and Vincent Benedict, the former, have a life-changing reunion. A key scene in the movie is when the twins get back together because it starts them on an improbable path of self-discovery and brotherly love.

In every aspect, Vincent and Julius are opposed; whereas Julius is tall, educated, and full of optimism, Vincent is streetwise, cynical, and physically intimidating. The twins have a strong bond and a strong desire to learn the truth about their origins despite their obvious differences.

When the twins do get back together, they have a tense and shocked first meeting as they adjust to the possibility of their strange bond. But as they spend more time together and go on several experiences together, they start to build a friendship built on admiration and respect for one another.

Vincent, as portrayed by DeVito, is a character that balances heart and humor while he works through the difficulties of his recently formed connection with Julius. His and Schwarzenegger's strong connection gives their on-screen interactions more nuance and realism as they set out to discover their real parentage and face future obstacles.

In the end, "Twins" shows how the twins' reunion may be a source of personal development and healing, as they discover how to value their special link and accept their differences. The character's journey from a cynical loner to a devoted and supporting brother is captured in DeVito's portrayal of Vincent, giving the touching film's ending more depth and emotional resonance.

6. The War of the Roses : DeVito's character Gavin D'Amato tells the cautionary tale of the Roses' turbulent marriage in the dark comedy "The War of the Roses," providing witty and perceptive commentary on the destructive force of love and ambition.

These classic sequences and characters highlight Danny DeVito's ability to evoke strong feelings in viewers long after the credits have rolled. DeVito's contributions to film and television, whether expressing serious and profound subjects or providing humorous quips, have had an enduring impression on the entertainment industry.

7. The "Chopsticks" Scene in "Big Fish" : DeVito's character, Amos Calloway, narrates the tale of a man who feels he can only communicate through the song "Chopsticks." This endearing and whimsical scene highlights DeVito's storytelling prowess and lends a magical quality to the movie.

8. The Taxi Reunion in "It's Always Sunny in Philadelphia": DeVito joined the show's cast in the second season, portraying the father of the main protagonists, Frank Reynolds. One memorable scene has Frank getting back together with Judd Hirsch, his former "Taxi" co-star, who makes a cameo appearance as his character's long-lost business partner, bringing back memories of their time spent together on the popular sitcom.

9. The Asbury Park "Danny DeVito Day" Parade: In appreciation of Danny DeVito's accomplishments in the entertainment industry and his hometown, Asbury Park, New Jersey, organized a parade in 2017 and proclaimed it "Danny DeVito Day." The parade culminated in a celebration that drew admirers and fans from all over the world, with floats, costumes, and performances inspired by DeVito's most well-known roles.

10. The Penguin's Speech in "Batman Returns" : DeVito's persona, the Penguin, makes a noteworthy announcement to the people of Gotham City about his plan to run for mayor and his vision for a better future. This moment demonstrates DeVito's ability to evoke charisma and terror, giving his portrayal of the enduring Batman nemesis more nuance.

11. The "War of the Roses" Climax : In this memorable and perceptive sequence from "The War of the Roses," DeVito's character Gavin D'Amato muses on the disastrous nature of the Roses' marriage. The film's darkly humorous examination of marital discord comes to a potent close with this scene.

These more legendary moments demonstrate Danny DeVito's range as an actor and his capacity to make an enduring impact on audiences via his standout roles and contributions to pop culture.

CHAPTER 8: THE ENTERTAINMENT INDUSTRY'S LEGACY AND ITS IMPACT

In the entertainment business, Danny DeVito leaves behind a legacy of lasting impact and cultural significance. With his skill, adaptability, and distinct personality, DeVito has shaped the entertainment industry and made a lasting impression on theater, television, and film throughout his illustrious career spanning several decades.

DeVito's legendary on-screen personas, which have enthralled crowds and won praise from critics, are a part of his legacy. From his breakthrough performance as Louie De Palma in "Taxi" to his iconic roles as Vincent Benedict in "Twins" and the Penguin in "Batman Returns," DeVito has demonstrated his versatility by emulating a variety of characters with nuance, wit, and realism. His performances have earned him a devoted following and cemented his place as a revered figure in popular culture. His name has become synonymous with his performances.

In addition to his talent as an actor, DeVito has made a lasting impression on the entertainment business as a director and producer. As a director, DeVito has brought his unique vision to life on the big screen, winning awards for films like "Throw Momma from the Train" and "Matilda." Through his production company, Jersey Films, he has championed innovative storytelling and supported emerging talent, producing acclaimed films such as "Pulp Fiction" and "Erin Brockovich."

DeVito's impact, however, goes beyond his work in front of and behind the camera. He has shared his knowledge and experience with the upcoming generation of talent, acting as a mentor and source of inspiration for innumerable budding performers and filmmakers. His support of significant social concerns, such as social fairness and environmental preservation, has also had a long-lasting effect, motivating other professionals to use their position for good.

Danny DeVito's outstanding skill, unshakable commitment, and lasting influence on popular culture characterize his legacy in the entertainment business. His unforgettable performances and his unseen contributions behind the scenes have left an enduring impression that will be felt by viewers for many years to come.

Danny DeVito leaves behind a vast and varied legacy in the entertainment sector that includes his outstanding work as an advocate, director, producer, and actor. Further facets of his legacy are as follows:

1. Cultural Icon : Thanks to his widespread recognition and adoration, Danny DeVito has emerged as a global cultural icon. His unique look, charismatic performances, and iconic roles have cemented his place in pop culture, with his characters and catchphrases appearing throughout popular culture.
Icon of Culture:

Danny DeVito's lengthy career in the entertainment sector has cemented his place as a cultural legend. Audiences all across the world have come to adore and appreciate him as a cherished figure in popular culture because of his unique character, dynamic performances, and endearing nature.

The cultural influence of DeVito goes beyond his on-screen personas. He has come to represent tenacity, originality, and innovation, encouraging followers to confidently follow their hobbies and accept their individuality. He is easily identifiable and adored by everyone due to his iconic stature and larger-than-life demeanor.

In addition, DeVito's popularity as a cultural icon spans generations and appeals to viewers of all ages. His ability to play a variety of roles, such as dark villains, funny misfits, or sophisticated antiheroes, has won him over admirers of all ages and solidified his place in the annals of entertainment history.

DeVito's influence in popular culture is further strengthened by his roles in memes, viral videos, and social media trends in addition to his contributions to film and television. The fact that his image and catchphrases are now widely used in online culture shows how influential and relevant his legacy is even now.

Danny DeVito's persistent appeal, ability, and charm have made him a cultural icon. He has made a lasting impression on popular culture with his unforgettable roles, legendary performances, and larger-than-life presence. As a result, his legacy will endure for many years to come.

2. Leader for Small Stature Actors : DeVito's triumph in Hollywood has opened doors for other small-statured actors by proving that charm and skill are not constrained by physical stature. As an inspiration to young performers from all backgrounds, he has fought against prejudices and promoted greater diversity and representation in the entertainment business.
Pioneer of Small-Status Actors:

Due to his career in Hollywood, Danny DeVito has blazed a path for diminutive performers, shattering barriers and dispelling misconceptions in a field that is frequently ruled by traditional ideals of physical attractiveness. DeVito has shown throughout his career that charm, talent, and adaptability are not constrained by height, opening doors for other performers to follow their passions in acting regardless of their physical characteristics.

Through his memorable roles, DeVito has demonstrated his ability to embody a variety of characters with depth, realism, and humanity, ranging from menacing villains to humorous eccentrics. His performances have gone beyond his size, bringing him praise from critics, accolades, and general acknowledgment for his acting prowess and adaptability.

Furthermore, DeVito's success has contributed to a shift in attitudes and opinions within the entertainment industry toward actors of modest size. He has encouraged young actors to follow their passion for performing and to confidently embrace their uniqueness by demonstrating that height is not a barrier to achievement.

DeVito's legacy as a trailblazer for performers of various backgrounds has been further cemented by his support for more diversity and representation in Hollywood, in addition to his accomplishments on screen. Using his position, he has promoted the abilities of performers with disabilities and pushed for increased recognition and opportunities for them in the business.

Danny DeVito's groundbreaking career has cleared the path for many performers of modest size to be included and represented in Hollywood. His accomplishments have broken down barriers, opened opportunities, and motivated actors of a later generation to follow their passions despite their physical limitations.

3. Comedic Genius : DeVito is a widely acclaimed comedian due to his unmatched comedic talent, expressive facial expressions, and razor-sharp wit. His contributions to comedy have left a lasting impression on the genre, inspiring a new generation of comedians and changing the face of comedic entertainment.

Funny Smarts

Danny DeVito's uncanny ability to inject humor into any role, along with his razor-sharp wit and perfect timing, demonstrate his comedic genius. Acclaimed as one of the finest comedic geniuses of his generation, he has captivated audiences with his irreverent humor, amusing escapades, and unique characters throughout his career.

DeVito's comedic genius is evident in his iconic roles, from his breakthrough performance in "Taxi" as Louie De Palma to his unforgettable portrayals in movies such as "Throw Momma from the Train," "Matilda," and "Twins." DeVito's characters are often quirky, capricious, and larger-than-life, and he brings his signature charm and charisma to each one.

DeVito also possesses unrivaled physical comedy talent; his expressive facial expressions, exaggerated movements, and comedic timing give every scene additional layers of humor. Casting as a charming misfit, a cunning schemer, or a foolish crook, he skillfully extracts humor from the most ridiculous circumstances, captivating audiences with his hilarious antics.

DeVito's contributions to humor go beyond his on-screen persona; he is also a director and producer. He has directed several comedies that stand alone as masterpieces, bringing his own unique aesthetic and caustic humor to every picture.

DeVito's off-screen persona enhances his humorous appeal in addition to his on-screen abilities. Known for his sharp tongue, humorous self-satisfaction, and contagious laugh, he has won over both colleagues and admirers with his easygoing manner and lively attitude.

Danny DeVito's comedic mastery has irrevocably changed the comedy landscape and delighted viewers everywhere. He has cemented his place among the greatest comedians of all time with his unforgettable roles, legendary performances, and unstoppable charisma, guaranteeing that his legacy as a comic genius will live on for many years to come.

4. Directorial Vision : In his role as a filmmaker, DeVito has explored dark comedy, satire, and human relationships with depth and delicacy. He has done this by bringing his distinct vision and storytelling sense to the screen. His directing has been praised by critics and

added to the diversity and depth of cinematic storytelling.

Vision for the film

Danny DeVito's distinct style of directing is defined by his fusion of sensitive storytelling, dark comedy, and visual flare. Behind the camera, DeVito has distinguished himself with his work by showcasing a sharp eye for detail and a unique style of cinematography.

With "Throw Momma from the Train," his feature film debut, DeVito proved he was a director with a keen sense of humor and a talent for fusing humor with serious subjects. The film showcases DeVito's humorous instincts and ability to experiment with unique narrative structures through its odd characters, offbeat humor, and deft plotting.

Similarly, DeVito demonstrates his directing vision in movies like "The War of the Roses" and "Death to Smoochy," where he skillfully strikes a balance between humor and a deeper emotional resonance. DeVito's directing gives the narrative levels of complexity and delicacy as these flicks explore the darker sides of human nature and the complexities of interpersonal relationships.

DeVito's use of vivid colors, attention-grabbing compositions, and creative camera angles define his visual aesthetic. Whether he's depicting the frantic energy of a carnival in "Matilda" or the cramped intensity of a broken marriage in "The War of the Roses," DeVito's visual storytelling gives his movies more depth and texture, which makes the spectator feel more fully immersed in the narrative.

Not only has DeVito directed movies, but he has also directed TV episodes such as "It's Always Sunny in Philadelphia," demonstrating his versatility as a director.

Danny DeVito's directing style is evidence of his inventiveness, cunning, and skill as a storyteller. Through his films, he transports viewers to both familiar and magical realms while deftly and perceptively examining the nuances of the human experience through humor, emotion, and striking visuals.

5. Philanthropic Activities : DeVito is well-known for his dedication to social causes and charitable endeavors. He has supported social justice movements, children's rights, and environmental preservation by lending his voice to several nonprofit groups. Others in the industry have been motivated to use their platforms for good by his action.

Philanthropic activities

Danny DeVito's charitable activities have improved several causes and organizations, demonstrating his dedication to changing the world and giving back to the community. Throughout his career, DeVito has contributed to numerous philanthropic causes and raised awareness of subjects near and dear to his heart by advocating for them with his resources and platform.

Environmental conservation is one cause that DeVito is deeply committed to. He has supported renewable energy, the protection of animals, environmental education, and many other activities that strive to safeguard the environment and advance sustainability. By encouraging other members of the entertainment business to use their platform for environmental activism, DeVito's efforts to raise awareness about environmental issues have helped to increase awareness and take action for the environment.

Apart from his efforts in preserving the environment, DeVito has been a strong supporter of children's rights and education. He has backed groups that give underprivileged kids access to chances and resources, such as mentorship, literacy, and art education initiatives. DeVito's dedication to children's causes is a reflection of his conviction that it is critical to raise the next generation and make sure every child has the opportunity to realize their full potential.

DeVito has also raised money and awareness for several health-related issues, such as cancer research and treatment, by using his celebrity profile. He has taken part in fundraising activities, charitable events, and public awareness initiatives that support medical research and help sick people and their families.

Danny DeVito's charitable activities have had a significant influence on society, bringing about good transformation and improving the lives of innumerable people. His commitment to children's rights, environmental preservation, and health-related causes is indicative of his empathy, compassion, and desire to improve the world for the coming generations.

6. Permanent Impact : Danny DeVito's impact on the entertainment sector goes beyond his creative output. He has fostered the next wave of performers and filmmakers by working with and mentoring up-and-coming talent. His creative impact will continue to influence future entertainment trends for years to come by encouraging originality and innovation.

Danny DeVito has had a significant and long-lasting impact on the entertainment business, changing popular culture, television, and movies for many years. His influence is seen in many ways, from his memorable concerts to his support of social concerns. He leaves a lasting impression on audiences and serves as an inspiration to upcoming artists and campaigners.

A contributing factor to DeVito's lasting impact is his standing as a cultural figure. Audiences all across the world have come to adore and appreciate him as a cherished figure in popular culture because of his unique character, dynamic performances, and endearing nature. DeVito is a multigenerational fan favorite whose classic roles continue to captivate audiences and solidify his place in the pantheon of entertainment legends.

More diversity and representation in the entertainment sector have also been made possible by DeVito's groundbreaking career. Being a small-framed actor, he has dispelled myths and torn down barriers, proving that charm and skill are not confined by physical attributes. Because of DeVito's success, young actors from all backgrounds have been encouraged to follow their passions and confidently embrace their individuality, which has increased diversity and representation in Hollywood.

Apart from his acting career, DeVito's involvement in directing, producing, and philanthropy has contributed to his long-lasting impact. He has tackled a broad spectrum of subjects and genres in his films, captivating viewers and provoking thinking with humor, passion, and striking visuals. DeVito's charitable activities have improved several causes by increasing public knowledge of and support for programs about health, children's rights, and environmental preservation.

Danny DeVito's talent, inventiveness, and dedication to changing the world are demonstrated by his lasting impact on the entertainment industry. His contributions to film, television, and society will be honored and remembered for many years to come because of his legacy, which will inspire and resonate with viewers for many generations to come.

Danny DeVito left behind a legacy of humanitarianism, cultural impact, and artistic brilliance. His campaigning and charity have improved society overall, and his contributions to theater, television, and film have made a lasting impression on the entertainment industry.

CONCLUSION

Beyond the confines of theater, television, and film, Danny DeVito's extraordinary career in entertainment has left an enduring impact. With his brilliance, adaptability, and unique personality, DeVito has enthralled viewers since his breakthrough role in "Taxi" and continued to do so with his legendary performances in "Batman Returns," "Matilda," and more.

DeVito has pushed the bounds of narrative as an actor, director, and producer by deftly and nuancedly examining themes of humor, humanism, and the human condition. He has become a cultural hero and a pathfinder for actors from various backgrounds thanks to his brilliant comedic timing, visionary directing style, and charitable activities.

Furthermore, DeVito's impact goes beyond his creative output. He has inspired people in the industry to utilize their voices for positive change by using his position to speak for significant social problems.

In conclusion, Danny DeVito left behind a legacy of humanitarianism, cultural impact, and artistic brilliance. For many years to come, audiences will be moved by his enduring influence, which will also serve as an inspiration to upcoming artists and campaigners.

www.ingramcontent.com/pod-product-compliance
Lightning Source LLC
Chambersburg PA
CBHW050234230526
45470CB00005B/1945